Born to be Wild
Little Wolves

Hélène Montardre

Words that appear in the glossary are printed in
boldface type the first time they occur in the text.

GARETH**STEVENS**
GS
PUBLISHING
A WRC Media Company

Playful Pups

Little wolves, which are called pups, spend all their time with their brothers and sisters. They love to chase and jump on each other, roll on the ground together, and hide from one another. As they play, they also fight and nip at each other. Some of the little wolves are stronger, **nimbler**, or smarter than the others. These pups know how to command respect, even when they play. When they are older and bigger, one of them will become the leader of the group, or **pack**.

A mother wolf has a **litter** of five to eight pups. The activities of the entire wolf pack revolve around taking care of the pups.

What do you think?

Why do little wolves always stay with their brothers and sisters?

a) Their mother tells them to stay together.

b) They get bored when they are alone.

c) They are afraid.

Little wolves always stay with their brothers and sisters because their mother tells them to stay together.

When wolf pups are born, their eyes are closed, and all they want is their mother's milk. Over the next few weeks, they open their eyes, learn to stand on their legs, and then leave the **den**. The pups play together in a group, which makes it easier for the adults to look after them and protect them when the pups are outside the den. Playing is a good way for the pups to get to know each other and learn how to communicate.

At one month of age, a wolf pup's eyes are blue. They will turn yellow when the pup grows up.

Little wolves are **cautious**, even when they play. They run to safety in the den as soon as they sense the slightest danger.

Playing together teaches wolf pups how to communicate with others. They learn about life in the pack and find out if they are strong enough to become leaders when they grow up.

Hearty Appetites

Little wolves drink their mother's milk for four to six weeks. Then the pups start eating pieces of meat, and sometimes fruit, that the adult wolves bring to them. Because the pups' jaws are not very strong yet, the adults chew the food first and spit it out for them to eat. All the wolves in the pack bring food to a mother and her pups.

What do you think?

Why do little wolves like to eat meat?

a) because they do not like the taste of vegetables

b) because their mother always tells them, "Eat your meat if you want to get bigger."

c) because meat is very important food for wolves

When adult wolves return from hunting, the pups jump on them and beg for a taste of the freshly caught meat.

Meat is very important food for wolves.

Wolves are **carnivores**, which means they mainly eat meat. In summer, a wolf hunts small animals, such as hares, rabbits, or rats, which it can catch by itself. In winter, wolves attack larger **prey**, such as **caribou**, elk, or deer. Hunting large animals is difficult, however, so the wolves in a pack hunt together. They look for the weakest animal in a **herd** and chase it until it falls down.

Wolves have powerful jaws that can grind up meat and bones.

When prey is too big to move back to the den, wolves eat it on the spot. Each adult wolf needs about 4 pounds (2 kilograms) of food per day.

Besides meat, wolves like to eat fish and frogs, and they will also snack on plants and fruits.

During winter, wolves travel long distances to find food. They walk in single file, placing their feet in the tracks of the wolf in front so they won't tire as quickly.

Growing Up Fast

By the age of eight months, a wolf pup is the size of an adult. It has a long, thin nose and short, rounded ears that often stand straight up. The young wolf now has slanted yellow eyes that reflect light at night — just like a cat's! Its legs are long and thin, and it can travel about 6 miles (10 kilometers) before it gets tired. Sometimes, a young wolf leaves its pack and stays away for a day or more.

The coats of wolves can be white, gray, black, or brown. The color of a wolf's coat depends on the animal's age, the location of its **habitat,** and the season. A wolf's coat is thick, so it keeps the wolf warm in harsh winter weather.

What do you think?

Why does a young wolf sometimes leave the pack?

a) because it has arguments with its friends

b) because the other wolves reject it

c) because it needs to get used to living alone

A young wolf sometimes leaves the pack to get used to living alone.

A thin layer of tissue over each of a wolf's eyes helps the animal see better in the dark. This tissue also makes the wolf's eyes glow in the dark.

When young wolves are eight months old, they have learned to hunt and are ready and strong enough to discover the world. Some young wolves have to leave their packs because new babies are being born, and a pack cannot become too large. A young wolf may move away when is about one year old. It will live alone, join another pack, or even start a new pack. In a few years, it might return to live with its family in the original pack.

This young wolf is off exploring the outside world. In the future, he might become the leader of a new pack.

All young wolves spend their first winter with the pack. Some leave the pack only after four or five years. Others may never leave.

Who's in charge?

Wolves communicate with grunts, howls, facial expressions, and body positions. The **dominant** wolves in a pack, for example, show leadership by pointing their ears upward and forward and holding their tails high. A wolf pack has both a dominant male and female. The other wolves in the pack are **submissive**. When they are near the pack's leaders, submissive wolves flatten their ears against their heads and hold their tails between their legs. Although a pack's life is organized around its leaders, all the wolves sleep, hunt, and play together and roam their territory daily.

What do you think?

Why does a wolf roam its territory every day?

a) to get to know it very well

b) to see if any strange wolves have entered its territory

c) to be reminded where the borders of its territory are

When the wolves in a pack come together, after being apart, they gather around their leaders. The wolves rub against and lick the pack's dominant male and female to show affection.

A wolf roams its territory every day to see if any strange wolves have entered it.

A wolf pack's territory is where it lives and raises its pups. Wolves mark the borders of their territories with urine or droppings. Marking the area is like putting up a "No Trespassing" sign. When other wolves sniff the scents, they understand that, even if there are no other wolves in sight, they are in another pack's territory. By marking their territories, wolves are able to avoid fights with other packs.

Wolves have a keen sense of smell. When they discover an unusual scent, they know that an unfamiliar wolf has passed by.

Scientists do not really know why wolves howl. Howling is one way, however, that wolves signal their presence to other packs.

A wolf is a fearful and cautious animal. By marking its territory, it leaves a scent that tells other wolves this area is already claimed.

Time for Mating

Mating season for wolves is mainly in January and February. Males and females begin approaching each other, however, at the beginning of winter. When mating season begins, all of the wolves in a pack become very excitable. Although they usually get along well together, young males fight with each other at this time of the year. Sometimes, they even start fights with the male wolf who leads the pack. Then the leader must prove that he is still the strongest.

Looking for trouble with the dominant female is not a good idea. She is quick to attack or start a fight with the other female wolves. When her wolf pups are born, however, the entire pack will take care of them.

What do you think?

Why do the wolves in a pack fight during mating season?

a) because only the strongest couple in the pack will mate

b) because wolves are jealous of each other

c) because wolves are bored in winter

The wolves in a pack fight during mating season because only the strongest couple will mate.

Many females in a pack could have babies, but only the dominant female will. Limiting the number of mothers is the only way a pack can survive. If a pack has too many pups, the wolves cannot take care of them all. When a mother wolf is almost ready to give birth, she prepares a den, using grass, moss, and her own soft fur to build a bed.

The wolf is a faithful animal. A male and female that mate usually stay together for life.

When wolf pups are born, they are deaf and blind and weigh about 1 pound (450 grams) each. They have small, rounded bellies, drooping ears, and short dark fur.

A female wolf carries unborn pups inside her body for about sixty-five days. As soon as they are born, the pups search in their mother's fur for her nipples so they can drink milk. During the pups' first days, the mother wolf will leave them only to get herself a drink.

Wolves are **mammals**. They live in forests and on plains and mountains and can be found in northern regions of North America, Europe, and Asia. An adult wolf weighs between 33 and 143 pounds (15 and 65 kg), depending on its habitat. Wolves live about ten years in the wild and up to twenty years in captivity.

Wolves are members of the dog family. They are related to foxes, coyotes, jackals, and even pet dogs!

A wolf has short ears that often point straight up.

A wolf's tail measures 11 to 20 inches (28 to 50 centimeters) long.

As a wolf grows from a pup to an adult, its blue eyes turn yellow and reflect light in the dark.

From its nose to the end of its tail, a wolf is 4 to 6.5 feet (122 to 200 cm) long.

A wolf has a keen sense of smell. It is able to detect the scent of unfamiliar wolves that have passed through its territory.

From the ground to its shoulders, a wolf is 23 to 35 inches (60 to 90 cm) tall.

A wolf runs about 20 miles (32 km) per hour when it is hunting. When necessary, it uses its strong, thin legs to run as fast as 35 miles (56 km) per hour, which is about the same speed as a car on a city street.

23

GLOSSARY

caribou — large deer that are related to reindeer and live in northern North America

carnivores — animals that eat the flesh of other animals

cautious — careful, not taking chances, or risks

den — a cave or hollow that a wild animal uses for shelter

dominant — having the most power or control

habitat — the place in nature where an animal usually lives

herd — a group of one kind of animal that stays together

litter — a group of young animals born at the same time to the same mother

mammals — warm-blooded animals that have backbones, give birth to live babies, feed their young with milk from the mother's body, and have skin that is usually covered with hair or fur

mating season — the time of year when male and female animals join to produce offspring

nimbler — able to move more quickly, lightly, and easily than others can

pack — a group of the same kind of persons, animals, or things

prey — animals that are hunted and killed by other animals

submissive — giving into the commands or control of others

Please visit our web site at: www.garethstevens.com
For a free color catalog describing Gareth Stevens Publishing's list of high-quality books and multimedia programs, call 1-800-542-2595 (USA) or 1-800-387-3178 (Canada). Gareth Stevens Publishing's fax: (414) 332-3567.

Library of Congress Cataloging-in-Publication Data

Montardre, Hélène.
  [Petit loup. English]
  Little wolves / Hélène Montardre. — North American ed.
    p. cm. — (Born to be wild)
  ISBN 0-8368-4440-8 (lib. bdg.)
  1. Wolves—Infancy—Juvenile literature. I. Title. II. Series.
QL737.C22M665   2005
599.773—dc22   2004058179

This North American edition first published in 2005 by
Gareth Stevens Publishing
A WRC Media Company
330 West Olive Street, Suite 100
Milwaukee, Wisconsin 53212 USA

First published in 2000 as *Le petit loup* by Mango Jeunesse, an imprint of Editions Mango, Paris, France.

Picture Credits (t = top, b = bottom, l = left, r = right)
Colibri: 22-23; J. L. Ermel 16(l); A. M. Loubsens 2, 4(b), 7, 12(t). Jacana: J/PHR Lepore title page, back cover, 6, 14, 22(l); Tom Walker 9(t), 19; Stephen J. Krasemann 10, 11, 12(b); Sylvain Cordier 18, 21. Sunset: Animals cover; Gérard Lacz 5, 8(both), 9(b), 13, 15, 16(r); H. Reinhard 4(t), 20(b); Leeson 17; Weststock 20(t).

English translation: Muriel Castille
Gareth Stevens editor: Barbara Kiely Miller
Gareth Stevens art direction: Tammy West

Printed in the United States of America

1 2 3 4 5 6 7 8 9 09 08 07 06 05